Shorelines

Other books by Bruce Lawder

Poetry
Little Choice
Shadings
Afterthoughts

Essays
Vers le vers

Shorelines

poetry by

Bruce Lawder

Homestead Lighthouse Press
Grants Pass, Oregon

Library of Congress Cataloging-in-Publication Data Pending

Names: Bruce Lawder, author.

Library of Congress Control Number: 2022943049

ISBN 978-1-950475-23-0

Homestead Lighthouse Press
1668 NE Foothill Boulevard
Unit A
Grants Pass, OR 97526
www.homesteadlighthousepress.com

Distributed by Homestead Lighthouse Press, Daedalus Distribution, Amazon.com, Barnes & Noble

Cover & Book Design: Ray Rhamey, Ashland, OR
Cover art by Gabrielle Lawder-Ruedin

Homestead Lighthouse Press gratefully acknowledges the generous support of its readers and patrons.

Notes and Acknowledgements

"The Sighting Of Orion" has its origins in a painting by Poussin. The painting in "Still Life With Fruit" is an invention of my own. I have taken the title of "Where Heat Looms" from David Mus's translation of André du Bouchet's *Dans La Chaleur Vacante*. The last lines of "Visit" are an inexact quotation from the final poem in Mark Strand's *Dark Harbor*. "Snow" and "Parallels" first appeared in *The Hudson Review*, "As Rivers Do" and "Elegy" in *Raritan*, "The Banker's Funeral" in *Salmagundi*, and "Where Heat Looms" and "Parallels" in German translation by Florian Bissig in the Swiss literary magazine, *orte*, as part of an article on my work.

Contents

For Gaby

I

Snow

I have hung odes on hawthorns
and elegies on brambles
and bound the wind harp
to the willow tree.

What will come of me now?
The snow
lies on the meadow, the branches
break in the wind.

As Rivers Do

You always wanted to invent yourself
after each failure and begin again,
much as a snake sloughs off its skin,
until we had to wonder what was left
for you to lose, or us. To start again….
I would have said: Beginnings have no end,
they go on in their deep and secret way
as rivers do, and leave their traces
even in drought, something to follow, continuous,
upstream or down, both to and from the source,
even when they jump the bed they've made –
something like that. But you'd moved on
to where you could not hear me once again
in the dark downward and abyss of shade.

Elegy

We saw them in their tattered rags of flesh, cowering
in corners, phantom-like, as if still half afraid,
half longing to come forward and to speak
with us, the new arrivals, in the dark,
as if we somehow held authority,
not they, the longer there, though equal now.
"We recognize the wrongs we have committed,"
one in our ranks began, as if he spoke
if not for all of us then more than one,
"and hope for your forgiveness if not trust,"
or so I thought he was about to say,
but then another shouted down the man
and afterwards another him, until like some
reverberating cave the dank and fetid air
grew void with voices. We the newly dead
had not yet learned the silence sacred there
and in confusion only cursed and stared.

Parallels

They run off together in twos, the lines, like parallel lives
on their way to wherever they have to go,
though they can cross each other, switching over
and off to somewhere else. From where I stand
you can travel to Rome, where all roads lead to ruin,
or overnight to Munich and then Dachau,
or ride the Lyria to Paris for the déjà vu.
No matter where you are, someone is waving,
wishing the one who is leaving a worthwhile journey
as the train screams out of the station and the rain
unexpectedly begins to fall like tears
blurring whatever it was
you thought you had wanted to see out there.
By now the waving has vanished along with the station
into a life you can only imagine.
Even the city has disappeared.
Choose, choose, say the wheels, and accept what happens
as what has to happen. Choose, say the tracks,
as the switches are thrown, there is no coming back
to the way it once was. Only think of that boy
looking down on the rails in the dark of the day
as the toy train threads the fixed landscape
time and again, and the lines, the miniature lines,
fine as cow spittle in the sunlit air,
repeat the promise that is everywhere.

Still Life With Fruit

It's often out of sight, the light source, though a window
might be present, up in the corner, in Vermeer,
or a light bulb hanging overhead in *Guernica*,
as if under whatever circumstances what stands painted
had not been invented but actually seen, even
if only for a moment in the mind's eye.
Picasso liked to paint at night to keep the natural light
out of the work – not that a falseness entered in,
call it a light of another kind, a light of another color,
a light of the mind, a seeing that can see itself
seeing. And while we're at it, why not more
than a single source, and from a multitude
of differing perspectives, all at once,
so that the shadows cancel themselves out
before our eyes, or at least seem to merge
into a background if not evenly lit
then equally in shade, as when
we hold two opposite ideas together
at the same time, not for their resolution
into something other than what they are,
but to keep the tension in the two alive,
the force between, that makes both feasible,
the two ends of one span, as with this table
by an anonymous Old Master long forgotten
on which against the black a single apple sits.

On Arrival

The parrots surprised us in the date palm trees
and the immaculate conception of the blank facades
so that at first no one among us noticed
the scent of sewage in the air.
We were late, of course, late once again,
and the welcoming committee,
as usual, failed to appear
as our tanks and trucks clattered into the city.
The only people we could see were looking down on us
from inside houses, as if alone the higher stories
offered protection. Only the children,
the hope of the future, waved. Somehow
everywhere souvenir shops had been left open
like wounds, as if whoever traveled now
went not forwards but backwards into a past
memorialized already into postcards. We saw then
that the parrots were wild and green and blended
their cries and colors into the shade
of the bladed palm trees and wondered
if wild as they were we still might teach
them a word or two of human speech.
But we had orders, and so descended
away from the square down to the water,
not sure if we would ever get things right.
Conscience, the polluted river, shone like light.

In The Dark

He stood there in the deep down darkness wondering
what to do next and what it was
he wanted. Not to see
the famous ones, not even
the poets or philosophers.
It was the women that he hoped
to speak with, and they came
as if of their own will, and not in dream,
breathless and beautiful,
forgetful, so it seemed, of what it was
that they had done, or not done, to themselves,
as well as others, and himself as well,
waiting for that oblivion said to come
after so many ghosting years.
He wanted to reach out to them,
as if the touching of itself
could animate the stillness of the place
and brush away each blurred and blunted look
revealing once more in the dark
as in a fountain's slowly outward flowing
the lean and vacant skies
pregnant with possibility.
One in particular he wanted to embrace
and in each other's arms and eyes
feel what they were, see what she had become,
what she had made of life and life of her.
Noli me tangere. He knew the rules. He broke them,
and of the other touched alone the air.

The Banker's Funeral

– for J.A.

"To be a famous American poet
is not the same thing as being famous."
So you say. I wouldn't know. What do the dogs care, anyway?
Those that don't know you bark as you walk by,
as do those that do. Does it matter?
The leaves have lost their color, which means
it must be somewhat later
than the season in mind. Why
hasn't the snow yet fallen as you thought it would
and will if you continue long enough? There is
still time to enjoy things as they are. Forget the dogs.
Forget the barking. What's the point
putting the muzzle of your nose in excrement?
Let the dogs do that. Look up: blue sky,
clouds dissolving the children's maps they made
if only for a moment. You're a big boy, now.
Time to enjoy the spare shape of the trees
that seem like markers on the way, but aren't.

Where Heat Looms

We knew that it was Orpheus, although
the man refused to share his name with us,
and just sat there in his dread-locks and shades
staring at nothing in the looming air.
From time to time he picked up a guitar
to sketch out something on the strings, as if
in answer to the little the birds did there.

                                                    He had
been doing this for years, the elders said,
coming and going in the town, and so
no one objected, publicly, or voiced their fear
of violence upon the waters or the street.
We knew the song he sang, should he sing it again,
would be of love, and loss, as it had always been
among the dark declensions of the light.
There was a woman with him that we thought the ghost
of what he sang, as if the song itself
had conjured her out of the arc and ash
and brought her forth a moment in the flesh
and flow of music high above the rocky gutturals
we were at home in, and too high to hear.
We asked him as politely as we could
to sing but not that song, only to play
upon the vacant promiscuities the promise of the day.

Revelation

– in düsterer Zeit

Think of John
on Patmos
in his cave,
athirst and hungry,
watching the waves,
or, outside, in the dark,
walking the water,
counting stones,
reading the rock
for what is written.

I have heard
the many waters
and a voice
beyond the waters.
I need no candle.
For I have eaten
of the shadow
like manna hidden
in the leaves of light
come down to earth.

I have my right
to the tree,
whatever
it may offer,
this life,
I may enter
through the gates
into the city,
a servant
not a slave.

Come, taste and see.
Here is root
and offspring,
fruit and flower,
the midnight
and the morning star.
Drink of the darkness
and be free
beyond illusion.

II

Album In Black And White

I

Garnets, in schist,
words in the woods
across the water:
blood from a stone.

The garnet mine
we called the cliffs,
seed pomegranates,
jewels rich as rubies.

We populated
the woods with red
men, saw in the fall
the land turn bloody,

then in winter the black
stain on the branch,
the bare
breath, and the stifling air.

II

O the beauty of lights
against the sky,
the clean
cuts of the architecture,
the lean
lines of the street,
the harp-
strings of the bridge,
dark water, and the long
leap to the other
side of the night.

See: how they free
themselves, now, the words,
in nothing more
than a sudden onslaught
of rain, blunt blurs
of color in the black
of things,
asphalt anthologies,
vocalic colorings,
mute mouthings, flowerings
of next to nothing.

O the wonder of rain
in the city, the cars
poling reflections,
the long
staves of the light,
pilgrims in darkness
crossing the water.

III

I know that some songs will never be heard, and not
only among the orders of angels, but here on earth, and that
a siren's wail or the fart of a truck will drown everything out

less than the casual clicks of computers or iPhones
or the selfies of couples kissing in public only to separate
and look at themselves, apart, on silent screens.

Nevertheless, I, too, have put on a blue suit, the one
you like me in, so thin its sheen
for some reason reminds you of moonshine,

something you hope to find in a poem one day,
so here it is, in this dark time, a word for you alone, the word
you have been waiting for, something at last to say.

IV

Clear out
the windows, prepare
the shops
for the holiday sale.

Screw the heads
on to the mannequins,
make sure the wigs
sit well.

Let them smile
with the fixed
and final
grin of the skull.

V

The plane is ready, it will take off
even if we aren't on it. But we are on time,
all we must do is get rid of our baggage.

I have my ticket, and you have yours, and so
there should be no problem in going through passport control,
we won't even have to stand in separate lines.

Look: somebody out there is shooting the rabbits,
somebody else is taking care of the birds
that otherwise might have disrupted our flight.

Now the harbor is going, so is the Statue, even the shelf
of a continent turns out to be nothing
if you take the high view, and regard the waves.

VI

See, in the streets,
the young
have begun
to juggle the ideas,
both large and small,
balancing everything
they know
of the apparent
impossibilities,
until they become
exactly what they have
to be, a momentary
and provisional
sketch of the real,
tossing whatever is
for the moment at hand,
crossing the necessary
contradictions, letting
nothing, absolutely
nothing, fall
to the ground. And now
someone is climbing
a ladder in the light,
leading another
up on the wires, and not
only one person,
many are rising
and in the empty
and open spaces
beginning to fly
on no more than a line,
and then
even that is let go....

Were we ever like that,
acrobats of desire,
falling and rising, leaping
each out of the other's
embrace, while the day,
another day, was beginning,
as it always begins,
in the impoverished
tents of the night?

VII

Breakwater rock,
the beach, the dark
waves, brightening, white
stone at our feet.

At night, to swim
the stars together,
parting the Milky Way
with no more than our hands,

then walk
the water's edge, as if it were
our diary, the page
torn free.

III

Notes From The Empire

Rain on a winter roof – no, the interval between two drops.

If absolutes must contradict each other, the only absolute is contradiction.

The Messiah is coming; the Messiah has come; there can be no Messiah: it must be the Word that hangs on the cross.

We have buried the dead in our minds. If you cannot see them, what evidence can be held against us?

The circle has become our symbol of perfection – no doubt because it contains the void.

The nice thing about space is that it keeps on going – so said the painter, limiting the canvas.

If nothing is impossible, everything is.

In the paradise of the real, the unreal reigns supreme.

From A To Z

To be the first and the last now is not to be the alpha and omega but only the A and the Z.

But how are we to pronounce the oceanic difference: A and Z, as in England, or A and Z, as in America? Even before the word the division begins.

A: the first word in the book – the indefinite article, no doubt as befits our status in these uncertain times.

ZZZ: the last entry, and not even a word – and this in only one language of many!

Between the beginning and the end, not only the words but the overhead lamp: grammar, syntax, subordination.

Say that a subject does something to an object through the agency of a verb – and the old psalm falls on deaf ears: Save me from the violent man!

Picture Book

Fall: the stained glass of the forest, illiterate still, the story.

If not a narrative a *Narrenlied*.

Blood in the leaves and the window in pieces.

The leaden pane in its branching, its breathing.

Somewhere out there you will find it, hanging from the tree.

The black fruit of the word.

A Letter

For some people all letters are black, for some people even vowels
have no color. For Hawthorne however the alphabet began with a
bloody flourish, the scarlet letter, initiated in an act of love found
shameful by the initial readers, and that shamed everyone, finally,
but the actual bearer. When I look at the letter A today, no matter the
color, what I see is how open it is at the bottom, as open as a wound,
how narrow at the top, how there is a bar between the gulf below and
the summit on high, and how the upper half of the letter – that which
is above the bar, the barrier – forms a perfect triangle, an equilateral
triangle, to be sure, equal for its members, though closed to the abyss
below even if supported by it. And what it demands, the letter, cries
out for, even, as every letter does, is the right, the freedom, to be read.

In The Country Of Pain

Pain, here, is still our daily bread: the staff and stuff of life itself. In every town we pass we see the signs: pain, everywhere, or almost everywhere, this kind, that kind. They are inventive now, the French, they have rediscovered their roots, the history of pain. Give us this day our daily pain, we hear, and forgive us the pain we have given to others as we forgive others the pain they have given to us. Even you, my darling, my faithful companion, my fellow traveler, must acknowledge the blunt facts of life in a shift of sound as we sit down once more to break our bread.

Paris

She sits there still in all her glory, the cathedral, her buttresses flung
outward like the oars of a trireme, the ship that must have brought
poor Paris to the city that still bears his name: archer and adulterer,
young adult and dolt, the one who would not face Achilles in a battle
but knowing of the otherwise immortal hero's mortal weakness let fly
the arrow from afar, and at the one place in the body where the angry
one was vulnerable, the place where, so says the song, he as a baby had
been held when dunked into the death-defying waters. Shunned by
his compatriots for what he had done, abhorred by the people he had
brought to ruin, he fled both homeland and adopted country ignorant
that the symbol of the city he would found and that one day would
bear his name – the city of lovers, the city of lights, of books along the
quais and picnics in the parks and below the sycamores beside the
river – would be this monument, this cathedral, stained with glass and
carved in stone, dedicated not to those partners in adultery, not to the
one said to have launched a thousand ships nor to the other fleeing in
a boat propelled by slaves, but to the harbor of all voyages, ship and
anchor at once, the merciful one, the Mother.

Limulus Polyphemus

Even as a child I did not understand the relation between the
horseshoe and the crab in the horseshoe crabs we found in the
backwaters of the Sound. I only knew that word and thing did
not fit together as I had imagined they should. For one thing, in
their carapaces and with their long tails they did not look like any
horseshoe I had ever seen. For another, they were and are not crabs.
We would find them in the brackish water when we waded through
the mud and sand, looking for clams, stepping blindly, painfully,
on their sharp and spiky backs or discovering their carcasses on the
abandoned beach, their insides hollowed out by the birds. Turned
over on their backs, horseshoe crabs alive look more like spiders, even
scorpions, than the crabs we knew from the local fish store. Later,
when I looked the word up in a dictionary, I learned to my delight
that the horseshoe crab is classified as a *Limulus polyphemus* and
that its Latin name comes from the large and apparently single eye
actually formed by the coalescence of a pair. It is named after one of
the monsters in Homer's great poem, in other words, for Polyphemus
is the name of the one-eyed giant that imprisons Odysseus and his
crew inside a cave, eating his men, two at a time, until Odysseus one
evening in an apparent and desperate offer of friendship gives the
monster some wine, introducing himself to the cyclops as Nobody,
and then, once the monster has fallen asleep, in a drunken stupor,
pokes out his eye by driving a red-hot stake into the socket. The
word itself, in Greek, means something like "abounding in songs and
legends" and in Homer's retelling of the story it is hard to imagine
how this name could be appropriate. When all the other one-eyed
monsters on the island ask the raging Polyphemus, himself the son of
Poseidon, the god of the sea, who has put out his eye and made him
cry aloud for revenge, the blinded one responds: Nobody has put out

his eye. Unable to find the source of his troubles, they turn back to
their own. And so among the cries for vengeance Odysseus and what
remains of his crew slip out of sight. And so it is with the horseshoe
crab that each day takes the word into its shell if not to walk on water
then to disappear below the surface, among the unheard songs and
legends of the sea.

Daedalus And Icarus

Daedalus wanted his son to follow in his famous footsteps and thus to pursue like the modern maze maker himself a career at the office.

Thus the warning to take the middle way, neither too close to the sun, lest he melt the wax in his wings, nor too near the sea, lest he wet his feathers and drown.

But the young man preferred his independence to a life of light behind glass, so runs the story, and thus refused to leave the labyrinth that for him was existence itself.

It was in fact the father who at work grew envious of what he took to be the freedom of the younger generation and so decided to try out the old wings.

It was in this way that Daedalus himself came too close to the son and, as a result, fulfilled the prophecy of his own story by falling from the sky.

At least this is the tale that Icarus now tells, the father of a son himself, and to preserve, he says, what remains of the family honor.

The Sighting Of Orion

The hero hunter in the mountains, gigantic, striding over the range of words: it must be Orion with his bow, but blind, and in search of something like himself.

Bees in place of the stars, flowery flames, infernal, the future constellation, but only in the darkness visible.

What seeds this time, then, cedes and accedes, if not vegetable gold, rooted in the dirt, internal, the darkest fruit.

There where the hero blindly if heroically strides there is nothing to see, nothing to climb or conquer, not even an abyss of his own making.

In a levelling age, the blind man tells himself, mountains have no choice but to become a fiction, and fiction a fact of life, colossal, though only for the small of heart.

Out of the subsiding sea, a shell, a future fossil, out of the fossil future, the re-discovered sea.

Snails

They carry their house on their backs, the snails, and are inseparable
from what they bear. Belonging nowhere, they are everywhere
at home, wherever they happen to be, even if in something like
perpetual motion, nomads adjusted to the seasons not the clock,
carrying their belongings as part and parcel of their being, their
belonging, in fact; and though there is danger everywhere, from above
as well as from below, they will not be turned aside from their journey
to wherever it is they are going, and, once there – if for them there is
a there – they do not stop but continue on their slow and steady way,
each in this age of discontinuities a monument to continuity. We can
only admire their perseverance, their insistence on going their own
way, free of our rules and regulations, passports and papers, nose
to the ground, and altogether down to earth, as they feel their way
forward.

Drawing On The Wall

In the cave that is a cave and nothing but a cave we grope in darkness
looking for a sign deep within the underground chambers, devoid
of light, feeling our blind way through what is still a river bed, doing
what we can to navigate the stalagmites rising from the dirt like
twisting towers of a Gothic chapel, ducking the stalactites overhead,
fingering our motion forward as we make our solitary way in a dark
as absolute as dark can be, ourselves no more than a series of sounds,
each to the other, footsteps reverberating in the void. This is a far
cry from the darkness that the Savior is said to have harrowed, far
from the depths the mother in the myth had to descend to find her
daughter, the taster of the forbidden seed. Cut off from the light,
without shadow, this is a dark that knows no parables, no legends and
no words, an unstoried dark, darkness itself, a world before the world
was written, and in that dark – and with not much more than a match
– we come upon what someone forty thousand years ago drew on a
wall and for no one to see, dark as it was then, too: the motion of a
hand, the curve of a muscle, a horn, a mark.

Granite

Granite is the bedrock here, thrust up millions of years ago as the earth's crust buckled in the fiery inferno and the inner fires raged beyond their limits, cracking open fault and fissure, folding rock on rock, and then subsided back into the earth, leaving what today we can take in our hands and not be burnt. Pick up a rock and you will hold a moment broken off from the mountain, a moment that for all the fiery inwardness of times long past can now be touched, a moment before anyone had even thought of separating one rock from another, or taught another human being how to say granite and not basalt, slate and not schist. For the rock in your hands comes from a time when even the word rock had not been invented, the world as we know it did not exist, the world of words where each word like a rock must displace another. What you hold in your hands, it turns out, is a piece of silence, a relic from another time, a time before time and our world were born. It speaks to you, if you can listen. And it is what you walk on, too, the bedrock of the place, the silent and ancestral story beneath your feet.

River Beds

The river beds run dry, the river beds run over. Even in the remotest regions removed from the industrious workings of the world we are ravaged by extremes these days, as in the world at large. There are times when we literally cannot cross over what is at our feet, when a small brook becomes a mountain torrent, where what we once considered stepping stones cannot even be seen in the discolored rush and roar of the current, and all we can do, if we venture out at all in such a weather, is to watch the mist rise from the earth like ghosts on the other side of the water. In summer of late the streams have begun to dry up, the water warms, alarmingly, the trout retreat, if they survive at all, and we can see the ruins that even brooks create: the sand-banks shoved aside, the gravel heaped where the current has turned away, the rock that once gave hole and hollow to the trout and nymph now isolated, high and dry, rough menhir stripped of rites. Strangest of all in such a time is to walk the river bed, to make our way downstream in the absence of the stream, as if a limit had been removed, a restriction, and we had entered a peculiar form of freedom, one not without its own pleasures, but new to us, as if we were ourselves the water.

Nettle Leaves

Many people regard the nettle as an enemy, having been stung at some point in life on their wanderings, and the equal of poison ivy in terms of painful consequences, and even those who know the delectable soup that can be made out of the leaves in spring often cut down the plant before it reaches maturity in summer, not wishing to be hurt again. Those that do so, however, fail to realize that they are also destroying the bed on which the Red Admiral lays her eggs, and so in protecting themselves from the stings and arrows of outrageous fortune they are also depriving themselves of one of the most admirable visitors you can have at home. Would it not be a better recipe for all the world to take the risk and let the nettles host whatever creatures come their way? Make your own soup, if you like soup, and let the butterfly have what is left of the plant. All you must do yourself is to step outside into the light to see it spread its fragile wings before your very eyes, free of the pale cocoon, and, frail as it is, paint the whole sky in its colors.

IV

Picture Book Tales

I

You were
always throwing yourself
out into orbit, a stone,
a storm, or one
of the songs to be sung,
in silence, to the storm,
the stone.
        And what
of the stand you took
when you stopped once,
in the middle of nowhere,
and stood as if alone
against the world, against
the way the world
seemed to be heading
in headless abandon,
        the dust
beneath your feet no more
substantial than a shelf,
and what you would not
do, what you refused,
someone else did.

Wasn't it something,
nevertheless, for you,
that time, among the words,
among the words and silences,
wasn't it something
not to have killed?

II

The living
die daily. But the dead
go on living, in us. They
who we say can not change
being dead change daily,
as we do. See: they are not
what they were, now,
when you first raised
your voice, not knowing
they could not be reached,
having no fixed abode.
                          Only the voices
remain in the air, faces.
But the sound that resounded
so fiercely once
it frightened fades now,
fades and withdraws
into a silence where,
breathless, they regard us,
the breathing, as we make
our way each day
forgetting them, forgetting everything
that happened, only to go on
in a necessary, an almost necessary,
blindness of oblivion.

Open your ears, then. See:
they are still there, observing us,
those we can speak to
only in silence, a silence
we the living sustain
only a moment, then
some noise breaks in,
we look up and
no one is there. It is

only another day, a day
much like another.
                          What was it then
that you wanted to say, to hear
them say? Can't you see
the trees are what they were,
rooted in dirt, the air
tangles itself in the branches
once again, where, like a thought
you did not know was there, a bird,
one of the great ones,
lifts itself from the dark.

III

Where have they gone,
the women, those you loved
and failed to love?
Into their own
lives, away from you,
as you from them.

Let the bookkeepers
balance the sheets,
it comes to nothing,
what you have done.
                          Who needs
a song? Another song? Go on,
pass through in silence.
Leave them the books.

Let it be night
again, let it be
the beginning of night:
a man,
or a woman,
alone,
sowing the air
with a handful of stars,
or was it stone
you took for seed,
a child's breadcrumbs,
furrowing a future
all the way to the salt
wash of the sea....

Even the bitter
leaves something sweet
now in the wake.

Better to walk
out, here, once more, one
among the many, alone,
under the darkening sky
of the country, where,
even if no one
listens, something
above us sings still.

IV

There was a chance,
then, of a face,
a real
one, and as simple
as that, across the table,

over breakfast, reading
the paper, or a drink
late at night, a look,
sudden, the eyes, the in-
comparable, unique.

V

I suppose there had to be someone insisting on pictures
of us together on vacation, social
media posts that showed us as a couple,
one or two bills, some party invitations,
someone insisting I inform on you.
"What is the color of your wife's toothbrush?"
"What is her favorite food?" And, in a rush,
"Tell me the name of every niece and nephew."

How I would love to sing in the land of the free
and the home of the brave this is our country
and yes, we, too, married for love. But what does it matter?
He asks how much money I have in the bank
and says if we aren't free to live together
at least you can go home – but not come back.

VI

Was it
only to empty air
we sang, then,
crossing the water,
only for funerals
we came together,
as if the country, what
we shared of it,
came clad in black,
mourning forever?

Absence
has grown into a further sense,
a presence
in which the voices
go on singing in us.
              And the ash
we sowed
deep in the furrows of the sea
now rises from a field
in the flight of birds.

VII

How much
of life we had
to miss, how much
we would have
to miss, the deaths,
the births
and marriages,
the long, slow illnesses,
the day by day.

See:
it was more
than the word, the thing
the word called up,
even apart –
the bird
on the branch, the
branch at the end
of the mind.

VIII

One day one of us
will vanish, and the air
will fill with absence –
there, where we walked,
in a presence still not
complete. Already
the birds fly off
as we approach, gulls from the sea,
the drought-struck leaves
blooden a little, in their turn,
and fade, in spring
the buds repeat the colors round the lake,
reddening.
                    Who would have thought
we would last so long? But weren't we always
preparing ourselves, reading
the leaves in order to be ready
for a moment beyond
pretense or preparation
when one of us will see
something of absolutely no significance
to the other, and no more
substantial than a few
traces in the first
of fallen snow
that even now
takes my breath away.

IX

Home
is where the heart
is, in a room
or in a palace,
a room
that is like a palace
when the heart is there,
the handicapped heart,
in a home for the handicapped.

The mountains ring us round,
they have the look
of waves, white-capped,
forever frozen
and about to break,
and what we see
from this island of exile
(that is no island)
is how the sea
breaks blossoms at our feet....

O sough and surf, O salt
reach of the night,
beads of the water
blown back, the white
stones where the black
waves curl
and do not crash!
Aren't we
now what we have
to be, star seed or dust,
substantial as the trees
entangled in the earth,
rooted in the dirt

and dark,
in our one double
downward and upward
individual plunge?

V

Homecoming

Arriving in the dark
I park the car
and stumble out
among the daisies –
how each spring they outsmart
the gravel in the drive
to flourish and survive –
and see the stars.

Night flowers. Fields of light.
And underfoot
the hurt earth gives
beneath the linden's
apparent symmetry,
the grass I have to cut.
I shall go down
myself into the dirt.

The Reaches Of The Real

It is a poor Vermeer
we keep here, the narrow
copper line of pots and pans
above the sink, the echo
color of the oak,
the black and white
tiles on the floor –
and, as always, the door
stands open, and the light
comes from a source
we can not see. Outside,
beyond the window,
dawn begins to rake
the dark aside,
shadow on shadow,
like broken sticks. The old
"let there be light"
comes slowly now.
We sip at coffee
as we watch and wait,
accustomed as we are
to such things here,
a frame, an opening,
and enter in.

Von des schimmernden Sees Traubengestaden her

– for Gaby

Sailboats upon the *Zürisee*,
peaked mountain whitenesses,
swans working their black feet
through the cleared water,
over our heads the Ferris wheel's
cage whirled, and underfoot
spilled cotton candy, crumbs
to walk the wood way home.

I still can see the fruit trees
in the water that breaks
these white petals, recall
the window wheel
of Amiens, the dark
rose window, in the barn,
the story stained with light
still starred in earth and straw.

What's our poverty now?
The iron wheel turns round
for each and every one
and overhead gulls scream
down shadow as they scavenge
the public walkway
where ads like standards
of some vandal army violate the air....

What's won lost must
be won once more, in time,
like breath, recovered,
as these blossoms that sing
what light withdrawn
now gives us back again, these white
beads, waves upon the water,
sails in the distance, summits, your birthday.

After Cythera

As when a cruise ship
pulls away from shore,
and everyone begins to wave
each to the other,
what they all know
is that the others grow
smaller and smaller
until nothing is left
to look at but the wake
between them, a dark
shredding of salt.

But where are we going,
so far from the shore,
they want to know,
those who in their hurry
forgot to question.
Where are the islands
with their beached allure,
the native customs
that we could admire
from our anchored position
and feel secure?

Shade

When the angel
appeared in the angle
of the shade and said,
ask of the dead
what you will, there
will be

no answer,
or, rather, the question
is all the answer
you will have,
so refine the question,
live with death a while,

he said
to himself, even if
it was only his own
voice in the void that he heard,
and the shade the shade
of the walnut tree,

and nothing
but that, it was all
that he would have
to take with him
into the winter light,
dark as it was.

He saw
then that the tree
was discarding its leaves,
that the shade itself
was becoming a mere
tangle of lines.

The angular angel,
or what he had taken for one
in that angle of darkness, said:
I told you so. You, too,
are no longer yourself
but everyone.

Reader With Owls

In the beginning
was the silence, in the beginning
was the cry.
It was going to be
a long night.

The moon
unnoticed had risen
to the window pane,
it shone like a lamp
onto the book.

He knew
that the cry
was the cry of the owl,
that it came from the tree
in the meadow.

It was not
one of the fabulous
trees in the book.
It was the ash-tree
in the meadow.

He turned
the page where the bird
had cried
and heard again
the familiar cry.

On the dark
side of the room,
and as if in reply,
came another silence,
another cry.

Local Color

The painting
would have to be more
than the pain
of painting, more
than the pleasure of purple
slashed with green.

The green
was new, it was
what made the rock
what it appeared to be,
the purple purple.
It was not you.

All winter
it had been nothing
but a drift
of gray on gray
bordering beige and black.
The green was new.

We knew
it was only the old
made new again
that made the rock
what it now was
and would have to be,

and not
the rock itself,
not even the rock
in all its stories,
at least as far
as the eye could see.

Ancestral Waters

As continental plates
drift slowly off
until all that remains
of what once held them
is no more
than the coastline
where we, too, stood,
watching the water
cast its white stones
forwards and backwards....

As if
out of the salt and slime
we came,
hoarding our words,
our weapons,
a choice,
or something like the right
of refusal was it
that set the feet
to wandering....

For birds
there are no borders,
the tree
roots where it is
the earth, and the branches
sprung to leaf
make possible the nest,
the scraps
that in shadow round out
a place to rest.

So we look out
from where we are
now, and what we see
is brought home to us,
summit and breaker,
whatever the weather
and no matter the country
that failed us or we fled,
the field in flower
and the clearing air.

The Salt Returns

The boats still stand
on crutches at low tide
in St. Guénolé's old
breakwater harbor,
the cold Atlantic swells
still slip and slide
out of our sight, a salt
air still assaults
what outside the chapel
remains of saint and devil.

So much for the figure!
So much for the legend,
the story! Remember?
Too poor a husband
to be your "sponsor",
I stood beside you looking west,
the black horizon
an iron bar, the barrier
even as man and wife
we could not cross....

It's all still there, the sand,
the salt, the loss
of land and language,
our dream and outrage,
as the indifferent, dark
waves beat against the rock
to fragment at our feet,
and what we thought
only a moment once
now and forever.

Visit

– for M.S.

So there you were
once more, in the plush
dining room chair,
raising the red
wine glass to tell us
how mistaken it was
to harbor the air,

and that wild thing
I took for a tree
in the darkening
down there in the dirt
was an angel, one
of the real ones,
about to sing.

A Note About the Author

Bruce Lawder grew up in Westport, Connecticut and now divides his time with his wife, the painter Gabrielle Lawder-Ruedin, between Switzerland and France. In addition to writing poems, stories and plays, he has also published critical articles on poetry and painting in the United States, France, Germany, Austria and Switzerland. He has a B.A. in English and American Literature from Dartmouth College and a Ph.D. in Comparative Literature from the University of Zürich. Before deciding to earn his living as a teacher, he was an actor at the Charles Street Playhouse in Boston, Massachusetts. He has published three volumes of poetry as well as a collection of essays on poetic structure, *Vers le vers*. His play *Computer Time* was performed by the American Theatre of Actors in New York City in the winter of 2022.

www.ingramcontent.com/pod-product-compliance
Lightning Source LLC
Chambersburg PA
CBHW022104020426
42335CB00012B/826